A Seagull Lunch
and
Other Nature Poems

A Seagull Lunch
and
Other Nature Poems

(Save Our Planet!)

S T KIMBROUGH, JR.

RESOURCE *Publications* • Eugene, Oregon

A SEAGULL LUNCH AND OTHER NATURE POEMS
(Save Our Planet!)

Copyright © 2019 S T Kimbrough, Jr. All rights reserved. Except for brief quotations in critical publications or reviews, no part of this book may be reproduced in any manner without prior written permission from the publisher. Write: Permissions, Wipf and Stock Publishers, 199 W. 8th Ave., Suite 3, Eugene, OR 97401.

Resource Publications
An Imprint of Wipf and Stock Publishers
199 W. 8th Ave., Suite 3
Eugene, OR 97401

www.wipfandstock.com

PAPERBACK ISBN: 978-1-5326-9066-2
HARDCOVER ISBN: 978-1-5326-9067-9
EBOOK ISBN: 978-1-5326-9068-6

Manufactured in the U.S.A.   JULY 17, 2019

Contents

Introduction | vii

Chapter 1   Nature's Creatures | 1
   1. A Seagull Lunch | 3
   2. A Magpie | 4
   3. A Bluebird Pair | 5
   4. In and Out Like a Flash! | 6
   5. The Race | 7
   6. Grizzly | 8
   7. When Eagles Soar | 9
   8. The Opossum | 10
   9. A Bird on Snow | 11
  10. A Triumphant Fox | 12

Chapter 2   Nature's Art | 13
  11. Nature's Art | 15
  12. Nature's Art at Dawn | 16
  13. Nature's Song | 17
  14. Colorful Thoughts | 18
  15. The Art of Beauty | 19

Chapter 3   Nature's Seasons | 21
  16. Seasons | 23
  17. Change of Season | 24
  18. Rust-Colored Leaves | 25
  19. Spring's Aromas | 26
  20. Springtime's Tease | 27
  21. The Crocus Knows | 28
  22. False Alarm | 29
  23. One Easter Morn | 30
  24. Release | 31
  25. Summer 1 | 32
  26. Summer 2 | 33
  27. The Summer Breeze | 34
  28. The Summer Rain | 35
  29. The Summer Wind | 36
  30. An Autumn Surprise | 37
  31. Autumn Colors 1 | 38
  32. Autumn Colors 2 | 39
  33. Autumn Hues | 40
  34. Frost | 41
  35. Bitter Winter | 42
  36. Mr. Wind | 43

Chapter 4   Nature and Imagination | 45
  37. Imagine | 47
  38. Imagine Rivers | 48
  39. As Rivers Run | 50
  40. Two Rivers | 51
  41. An Ocean Wave | 52
  42. Shifting Sand | 53
  43. Surprise | 54
  44. What Does a Flower Mean? | 55

Chapter 5   Nature's Gifts | 57

   45. Nature's Gifts | 59

   46. An Enchanted Wood | 60

   47. A Little Oak | 61

   48. The Plains | 62

   49. The Oregon Coast | 63

   50. Mount Kilauea | 64

   51. Wonder | 65

   52. Mountains | 66

   53. A Mixture of Colors | 67

   54. Nature's Birthday Card | 68

Chapter 6   Nature's Demise | 69

   55. No Autumn Time | 71

   56. Climate Change, a Myth? | 72

   57. Global Warming | 74

   58. Where Is the Rain? | 75

   59. Which Trademark? | 76

   60. Greenland, for You We Grieve | 77

   61. Disappearing Ice Castles | 78

   62. Suppose | 79

Introduction

WHAT IS MORE EXCITING than a walk along a forest trail, an evening sunset stroll along a sandy beach, a moonlight sail down a bay, a soaring flight above a glacier, the sound of a whippoorwill by morning light or a nightingale at dusk, a hike along a mountain trail, a swim in a fresh-water stream? One can go on and on with delightful descriptions of nature experiences. It seems that the moment one experience is described another transpires, sometimes taking one's breath away.

I have been fortunate in my life to travel through many countries of the world and to behold amazing wonders of nature. In Nepal, I have seen the splendor of the mountains and been astounded at how nature provides the network of life for small villages and towns. I have watched the domesticated, majestic Brahminy bulls in India tolerate dire heat and even drought with astounding stamina, almost impossible to humans. At the Masai Mara Game Reserve in Kenya I once saw the annual migration of the Wildebeests from Kenya to Tanzania and asked myself, "What does nature know that I do not?" There also I marveled at the freedom of animals I knew in my youth only in domesticated zoos: giraffes, antelopes, zebras, hyenas, etc. Along a river in Bangkok I have seen huge schools of fish that would burst a net if one were to try to catch them all at once. I have seen the reborn herds of buffalo in some of the US western National Parks and wondered how these regal animals could possibly have approached extinction? At the Jarong Bird Park in Singapore I was amazed at the scores of species of birds from around the world graced with a gorgeous breadth of colors. Many are stunningly beautiful. In East Malaysia, I have stood in awe at the foot of Mount Kota Kinabalu with its snow-capped top. In Mongolia, I have gone to the edge of the Gobi Desert and been struck by its breathtaking beauty and indescribable vastness. Nearby, I have seen innumerable herds of horses, camels, and yaks, so characteristic of one of the last, but diminishing nomadic cultures.

I remember a Boy Scout trip as a teenager that took me to the wonders of Carlsbad Caverns and Mammoth Cave. In the latter, in a river flowing deep below the earth's surface I saw a fish with no eyes. Mother Nature had simply adapted this fish to its circumstance of total darkness where eyes were not needed.

INTRODUCTION

As a young boy, I adored a Boston Bulldog I owned, who in contrast to most other dogs had one blue eye and one brown eye. I was extremely curious when she had a litter of eight puppies whether one of them would have eyes like the mother. Much to my disappointment all of their eyes were brown.

On one occasion as a young man, a state conservationist enlisted my assistance to mark trees in a forest for cutting. While I had learned to identify many trees and their species in a high school botany course, I marveled at how many more trees I did not know and could not identify but my conservationist friend knew the name of each one we marked or passed by.

By now perhaps it is clear that I have had marvelous encounters with nature throughout my life. Some of the more intimate encounters are described in the poems of this volume. Many of them are simple descriptions of the wonders of nature. Some address the tragedy of nature's suffering caused by human thoughtlessness and negligence. Others are a response to the magical change of seasons, a cycle which transforms the colors of the earth's foliage, brings the advent of animals' change of habitats, along with hurricanes, monsoons, and other storms. From one season to the next the earth bears fruit, yields crops, and its meadows bloom.

One group of poems (6–7, 53–56) was precipitated by a trip across the vast expanse of Canada with its radically changing landscapes, its multiplicity of fall leaf colors, and its varied population of animals.

Many of the poems are from real life experience, while others are products of my imagination peaked by nature's numerous gifts. Nature is one of the most precious gifts human beings have. It is for enjoyment, sustenance, and preservation.

> Job. 12:7–8:
> "But ask the beasts,
> and they will teach you;
> the birds of the heavens,
> and they will tell you;
> or the bushes of the earth,
> and they will teach you;
> the fish of the sea will declare to you."

Some of the poems (56–62) offer words of caution about human carelessness in preserving nature and its wonders. In another section of poems, I write about nature's enchanting seasons. But do we ever pause to consider

INTRODUCTION

what it would be like if the advent of autumn, or any other season, no longer came? Yet, the truth is that in some parts of the world autumn already ceases to appear. Once fertile lands are now barren wastes and hills once populated by trees and plant life bear nothing except, perhaps, stubble. Gushing rivers and flowing streams are no more. We must ask: Do we want this fate for the rest of the world when we know there are things that human beings can do to slow and turn the tide of climate change?

We cannot stand idly by in silence when there is proven scientific evidence that *destructive climate change is a reality*. Shall we do nothing about: the elevation of worldwide temperatures, the rising of ocean levels that could eventually destroy some island nations and their inhabitants, the loss of farm land and crops, the steady crumbling of glaciers and ice caps that forebode the demise of sea life and its food?

> Will there be winter, spring next year
> and what of summer, fall?
> Will loss of seasons cynics sneer?
> Will they have that much gall?

A major source of the diverse problems we face is simply greed. How can we possibly believe the illusion that the retaining of the production of fossil fuels for the sake of jobs is sustainable? The evidence of science clearly proves that the increase of carbon dioxide and greenhouse gases precipitated by the increased use of fossil fuels gradually does irreparable damage to the ozone layer of the atmosphere surrounding the earth. This could eventually lead to the demise of the conditions for life sustenance.

Throughout many parts of Africa, one already sees the decrease of rainy seasons which foster the growth of food for humans and a vast array of animal life, as well as the sustenance and rebirth of forests. The human handprint of greed is seen on nature across the globe. God forbid that the days come when we can no longer enjoy the delightful sound of raindrops on a roof or enjoy a bird sipping water at a stream's edge.

People and nations must rise and say, "No more." We will commit the funds, energy, and effort to turn the tide. We will initiate programs for a green world with a plethora of jobs, even though they require re-training of a work force, to replace outdated jobs that ultimately harm nature and our world. We will preserve the beauties of nature for our enjoyment and their aesthetic elegance. We will preserve the forces of nature that sustain life and make life worth living.

Chapter 1

Nature's Creatures

1. A Seagull Lunch

A seagull dipped into the sea
    to catch its noonday meal.
I watched him dive quite forcefully
    and come up with an eel.

The eel was jumping to and fro
    within the seagull's beak;
but he held on, would not let go,
    displayed seagull technique.

The seagull flew swiftly away
    the noonday meal he'd caught:
an eel to his surprise his prey;
    a fish is what he'd sought!

2. A Magpie

A solo magpie stares at me
outside my window from a tree.
It moves its head as if to say,
"Have you no food for me today?"
It waits and waits for my reply;
It's perched as if about to fly.
Because it has no action seen,
it flies off to another scene.

3. A Bluebird Pair

Two bluebirds landed on my fence
    just after noon today.
They tarried, sunned not flying hence,
    to catch each sunbeam's ray.

How clear it was they were a pair
    with space for two it seemed;
the female was content to share.
    The male's bright colors gleamed.

The sunlight warmed them as they preened
    the ruffles at their throat,
and one upon the other leaned,
    then preened the other's coat.

4. In and Out Like a Flash!

When I came in my own back door,
    I was amazed at what I saw:
A chipmunk dashed across the floor!
    Yes, you are right! I stood in awe!

I was dismayed at what to do,
    I did not want my cat to see;
I knew he'd want to bite and chew
    the chipmunk to eternity!

Alas, I left my door ajar,
    and out the little fellow ran.
Where did he go? I'm sure quite far.
    He seemed to fly like Peter Pan.

5. The Race

I watched a chipmunk scamper by
    that swiftly raced right through a field.
He did not seem the least bit shy,
    at least his nature that revealed.

Just then a field mouse crossed his path;
    the chipmunk for a second paused,
then turned and mustering his wrath,
    started the chase his instinct caused.

They raced through grass and tumbled sage;
    the field mouse ran this way and that.
There was no way that I could gauge
    who'd win the race or just fall flat.

Just then an old tomcat appeared.
    The mouse, the chipmunk dashed away.
The monster they had always feared
    postponed the race, that's what some say.

6. Grizzly

Wherever there's a passing stream,
    an otter swimming by,
a bear is fishing, it would seem,
    for salmon, the sockeye,

A deer unnoticed joins the scene
    and dines on berries blue.
A mother raccoon is quite keen
    to feed her babies too.

And then a grizzly bear appears
    and roars a frightful sound.
Each animal then disappears,
    just grizzly's left around.

7. When Eagles Soar

When eagles soar into the sky
    above a hummock green
to granite cliffs that are nearby,
    how exquisite the scene.

Two soon part ways and make their dives
    descending to the plain;
their claws are poised like sharpened knives
    to snatch a baby crane.

With breakfast caught, they soar again
    to cliffs where their nests lie,
and hungry eaglet mouths all strain
    to quell their hunger cry.

The parent eagles then alight
    with food for all to eat.
The eaglets filled with such delight
    start singing, what a treat!

8. The Opossum

I came upon an opossum
    that from my presence fled,
and then beneath a rose blossom
    lay down as though were dead.

I'd heard this creature death could fain
    to fool a threatening beast;
to me, however, it was plain
    this 'possum wasn't deceased.

I hid behind a big oak tree
    so I could slyly wait
to see how soon he'd try to flee.
    My absence was the bait.

As soon as I could not be seen,
    his eyes were opened wide;
his was it seemed, a grinning mien,
    as he ran off to hide.

9. A Bird on Snow

A bird did on the snow alight
    as I walked into town.
It pecked the snow without affright,
    though I stopped and looked down.

He pecked and pecked close to my feet;
    I stared with some surprise.
I must admit it was a treat
    to watch him seek a prize.

Just one small piece of grain his beak
    was longing there to find.
My, would it indeed be chic
    to know what's on his mind.

This bird let me stand close to him,
    while he looked for some food.
Most birds would start without a whim
    and fly away for good.

I stood and watched for minutes long
    until beneath the snow
he found a peanut, sang a song,
    and off my friend did go.

10. A Triumphant Fox

A fox, raccoon, and rabbit meet
    along a forest lane.
The rabbit quickly feels the heat,
    then suddenly there's rain.

The rabbit, raccoon dash away,
    the fox just stands his ground.
Quite feeling that he'd had his way,
    the fox just struts around.

CHAPTER 2

Nature's Art

11. Nature's Art

Vast snow-white clouds with skies of blue
and white-capped seas of emerald hue
embrace the earth from East to West,
while rainbows show heaven's treasure chest.
This treasure chest, whose colors grand
emerge across the varied land,
paints autumn leaves, peaks capped in white.
They're nature's art, borne to excite,
excite emotion and the heart,
elation that will never part.
If humans would but pause and feel,
the joy of nature's art is real!

12. Nature's Art at Dawn

The morning horizon lay still against the sky,
as a glimpse of shimmering orange
touched its quiet, motionless edge.
Slowly, as if it nothing could disturb,
nature's broad brush of bright orange
stretched across the morning sky and
diminished the remnant of the moon.
Clouds emerged, as if from nowhere,
covering the rising sun with a cloak of white,
turning shimmering orange into a translucent veil.
Suddenly a high, blustering ocean wind
whisked nature's momentary seascape away,
and the blazing, morning light of the sun
spread its vast rays across nature's canvas—
the horizon, the sea, the clouds, the sky.

13. Nature's Song

Creation rings through hills and dales
    with nature's joyous song;
the gentle wind and hearty gales
    rush all the strains along.

The trees whir with a haunting sound,
    the leaves a cantilen',
and trickling, bubbling brooks resound
    a rhythmical refrain.

There's music in an evening breeze,
    a shooting star's bright glow;
with nature's rhythm one's at ease,
    its music's steady flow.

There is a symphony of sound,
    if one will pause to hear.
There is a concert all around
    from nature's music sphere!

14. Colorful Thoughts

Red, yellow, white, blue, pink, and green,
    these colors spread their hues,
as springtime's flowers paint the scene
    and change a hillside's views.

No colors in the world? How dull!
    With rain even deserts bloom,
and ocean plants by an old hull
    for colors soon make room.

Above the earth or far below,
    there's color all around.
Refuse to look—we'll never know
    the colors that abound!

15. The Art of Beauty

How dull the soul that cannot see
    the beauty that it passes by:
A mountain peak, a brook, a tree,
    a desert wadi, dry.

The valleys, rivers flowing free
    across a wide terrain,
the heather on a hill, a lea,
    rain forest's sudden rain.

How can such beauty be ignored
    by any human soul?
How breathtaking a glacier, fjord,
    ice plains near the North Pole.

Pass all these by, life will be dull,
    for beauty is the art
that makes the lives of humans full,
    the pulse of every heart.

Chapter 3

Nature's Seasons

16. Seasons

I would not live without snowfall,
    without the leaves whose colors change!
If summer's wind should never call,
    spring had no flowers! Oh, how strange!

The seasons—nature's gift they are,
    the human spirit's moods to woo:
to light the heavens, to see a star,
    and in a rainbow every hue.

I want not one of them, no, all:
    snow, rain, the sun, and lightning too.
So, summer, winter, spring, and fall,
    I'm ready for gray skies or blue.

17. Change of Season

The trees are straining to burst forth
    with buds that foretell spring;
with winter's cold wind from the north
    the birds do not yet sing.

The songs of birds are a sure sign
    that spring is on the way:
On grains and berries then they dine
    amid the tree buds play.

But winter cannot hold spring back,
    although its will is strong,
for nature's order stays on track,
    spring flowers are never wrong!

The change of season to the next,
    the winds, storms, snow, and rain,
may make a few folks quite perplexed,
    while others don't complain.

18. Rust-Colored Leaves

Outside my window leaves of rust
    shine burnished by the sun.
The lower ones are glazed with dust;
    the crows are having fun.

The higher, shining leaves catch light
    that shows their every vein,
their sparkle in the sun so bright;
    they weave a color skein.

Would I could sit here all the day
    till dusk would sunlight dim,
and evening wind would start to play,
    and dance and dance with them.

19. Spring's Aromas

Aromas o'er my garden waft,
    from roses like perfume,
and down the valley there's a croft
    decked out in spring's costume.

A costume of wild flowers fair:
    Sweet honeysuckle vines
perfume the valley's gentle air.
    Yes, it's "dressed to the nines."

"Dressed to the nines" with Queen Anne's Lace
    and pink-bloomed clover too,
while rabbits through bluebonnets chase
    and springtime's born anew.

Such sweet perfume one cannot buy;
    it cannot be produced.
It's nature's own natural high
    by which we're all seduced.

20. Springtime's Tease

How biting yet the winter breeze,
preventing springtime's slightest tease.
With snow's demise the peeking sun
attempts to show that spring has won,
has won the annual season change.
If not, trees, bulbs will find it strange.
Quite strange? Oh yes, quite strange indeed
for grass and flowers find a need
to blossom forth in sudden bloom
and cast aside earth's wintry gloom.
I'm ready too for spring bird's song
to cheer me as I walk along.

21. The Crocus Knows

The crocus knows when winter's past
    and springs up from the earth,
and other plants that seemed asleep
    emerge with a new birth.
Their foliage dances in the sun,
    their stems majestic rise,
and colors from earth's blooming flowers
    stand out as nature's prize.

The lilies of the field they grow
    and neither toil nor spin,
and even kings are not arrayed
    with beauty found therein.
Such beauty merits deepest awe,
    respect, and watchful care,
If not, the damage nature bears
    will be beyond repair.

What does this cycle say to us—
    rebirth from winter's sleep?
All nature soon reveals the clue
    to life that we may reap,
for we like plants may wake anew
    from winters of our strife,
and spread the hues of joy and hope:
    the reawakened life?

22. False Alarm

The sky is gray, there is no sun;
the thunder rumble's just begun.

Will there be hail and flooding rain,
a storm to test a weather vane?

An hour ago, the sun was out;
it seemed as though we'd have a drought.

But now the threatening, dark black clouds
have scattered all the beach-bound crowds.

I'll take my sandals, my beach wrap
and go and take a pleasant nap.

23. One Easter Morn

One Easter morn I can't forget
    when I was young and green.
I've been forever in its debt
    for a breath-taking scene.

As I approached a small hill's top
    with awe I was o'ercome.
A burst of colors made me stop;
    an apple tree, a plum

in pink and purple both were dressed,
    divine indeed the smell,
with which azaleas too were blessed,
    Oh, I remember well.

Wisteria and tulips too,
    gardenias, roses red,
were on that Easter morn in view,
    with dazzling colors spread.

Yes, this is Easter-time, rebirth,
    and nature wants to say,
"If you but gaze across the earth,
    each day is Easter day."

24. Release

Hurray! Above the freezing mark
    the temperature has risen!
Will you allow me the remark?
    "We're out of winter's prison!"

The waning of the winter's snow,
    and daily clouds of gray
tell plants, "It's spring, and you may grow.
    You must not wait till May!"

So, lovely April, bring your showers
    and heather on the hill.
We've waited long to see your flowers,
    your colors, what a thrill!

25. Summer 1

The summer mountain air is fresh,
    so too along a sandy shore,
where jet streams with sea breezes mesh
    to lift the spirits more and more.

With winter, springtime both now past
    the summer season has its turn,
its upbeat different mood to cast
    on all who for warm sunshine yearn.

To swim and sail, what a delight!
    How I recall them from my youth.
Vacations, trips, a new camp site,
    a summer dance, a girl named Ruth.

The nightingale, whose song I heard,
    would evenings just at dusk appear.
While summer's warmth still in me stirred,
    it charmed me as it did last year.

How well we know a season change
    can alter our demeanor, mood.
How wise it is life to arrange
    so joy each season will include.

26. Summer 2

The summer sun kisses the earth
    with warmth winter knows not;
the ground with seeds and bulbs gives birth—
    the first "forget-me-not."

What is in store this year in June,
    since April, May, brought rain?
Shall we await a harvest moon,
    crop blossoms on the plain?

Wild roses on a lonesome road
    color the green terrain,
and clover's pink-white stylish mode
    will make no one complain?

In summer nature wears a dress
    of color, foliage fair,
and passers-by are free of stress,
    embraced by nature's flair.

27. The Summer Breeze

The summer breeze wafts gently by,
    a touch upon my cheek;
its winsomeness I can't deny—
    my hair style makes quite sleek.

The way it fluffs a seagull's back,
    and smooths the summer sand,
reveals dear Mother Nature's knack
    for managing her brand.

If I could sit here all the day
    with this exotic breeze,
it certainly could have its way—
    with me, just me to please.

28. The Summer Rain

The summer rain is not like May;
    the torrid heat turns it to steam.
On blazing asphalt, it can't stay,
    but changes to a misty stream.

It rises to a higher sphere,
    perhaps into gray clouds or white,
and there if lightning should appear,
    returns as rain by day or night.

29. The Summer Wind

What can one say of summer wind,
    a breeze from off the bay?
Its pleasure I shall not rescind;
    I'll treasure it today.

Upon the cheek, a gentle touch
    of Mother Nature's kind,
is never for my moods too much.
    Oh no, that I don't mind!

Strong stormy winds in summer time,
    are not a welcome guest.
Folk brace themselves in every clime,
    such winds give no one rest.

So, summer wind, bring calm and peace;
    inspire a tranquil mind.
From storms and gales give us release.
    This summer, please be kind.

30. An Autumn Surprise

A winding road took me today
    high up a mountainside,
and nature took my breath away
    as sunshine was my guide.

It struck the golden, shining leaves
    and others brown, rose-red,
a color scheme that nature weaves,
    when sun and colors wed.

The light's refraction through the trees,
    like streaks of shooting stars
created sights one rarely sees.
    Could this compare to Mars?

It was an other-worldly scene,
    a transport of delight,
and should it not again be seen,
    it was a wondrous sight.

31. Autumn Colors 1

A quilt of colors cloaks the trees
    when we reach autumn-time.
Their leaves float gently down with ease
    when autumn's in its prime.

They float from branches to the ground,
    a blanket cover rich
with rainbow colors all around
    to fill the smallest niche.

We tread the leaves or toss them high,
    while children make a pile,
and jump on it, as if to fly,
    then landing with a smile.

The multi-colored painted leaves
    reveal that nature's art
in them aesthetic heights achieves,
    that make us all take heart.

Take heart that summer now is past,
    for autumn's birth is wise,
its colors for a time will last
    and fill us with surprise.

32. Autumn Colors 2

When autumn-time comes into view,
    before leaves start to fall,
it is as if trees stand in queue
    to paint leaves, large and small.

The colors like a rainbow stream,
    some muted, some quite bright,
by sun or moon project a gleam
    that lasts both day and night.

The wind invites the leaves to dance
    and swings them, to and fro,
so, every color has the chance
    each nuanced hue to show.

The multi-colored world of fall
    embraces us each year
as Mother Nature drapes her shawl
    of color round earth's sphere.

So, drink them in, these colors all,
    pastels and oils, they seem,
for nature has the wherewithal
    to make its palette dream.

33. Autumn Hues

Last autumn, just a year ago,
    when green leaves all had turned,
to mountains, valleys down below,
    rich beauty then returned.

The red, the pink, and yellow hues
    oft took our breath away.
No matter whence our many views,
    we knew, the hues can't stay.

How happy were the moments we
    imbibed this beauty fair.
If only we in autumn see
    the colors that are there!

In spring, the many-colored flowers
    are breathtaking to see,
but autumn's leaves have similar powers:
    enchanting, we agree.

34. Frost

The frost at dawn its blanket spreads
o'er rooftops, grounds, and flower beds.
It sparkles in the morning light
and summer's green is out of sight.
It crackles under feet when cold
and melts as soon the sun is bold.
It vanishes with warm degrees
but reappears winter to please.

35. Bitter Winter

It's colder yet, the snow still lies
and winter still wears no disguise.
Like chilling breath its freezing wind
reminds you how the air has thinned.

Yes, it can take your breath away.
Just one quick blast and then you sway
from left to right, then forward, back.
Your face feels it, the blast, a whack!

Oh, bitter winter, wield your power,
but for the coming, trying hour
just ease the wind a bit for me;
then I'll get home and let you be!

36. Mr. Wind

The wind blows fiercely in my face,
    as if quick to remind,
though snow has left nowhere a trace,
    winter has its own mind.

And furthermore, the wind is not
    to wintertime confined.
It seasons shapes with many a plot,
    both pleasant and unkind:

Light ocean wind, a summer storm,
    a gentle autumn breeze,
and hurricanes in every form,
    the cyclones that down trees.

But, Mr. Wind, though winter still
    holds springtime yet at bay,
If you would show me your kind will:
    Give me a pleasant day!

CHAPTER 4

Nature and Imagination

37. Imagine

How sleek and slender are the trees
    shaped in a silhouette,
as if they were an ancient frieze
    upon a parapet.

The background's filled with snow-white clouds;
    the foreground's filled with stars.
The wind whirls leaves like dervish shrouds
    to faraway red Mars.

Who can imagine such a scene?
    Is it not but a dream?
Is there before my eyes a screen
    to change things as they seem?

Imagine things not as they seem;
    imagine what is not!
Life then will be no boring scheme,
    no matter what you're taught.

38. Imagine Rivers

When standing by a river-side,
   a wisp of wind-blown spray
began imagined thoughts to guide:
   Had Pharaohs come this way?

Is this the mighty, flowing Nile
   that ancient armies crossed?
Did Moses the Red Sea beguile
   till Pharaoh's cause was lost?

Is this the Elbe, Charlemagne
   drove Saxons through by force?
The Amazon where tribes campaign
   to stay the river's course?

Is this the Niger, Congo too,
   where soldiers still make war?
Are treasures there the world should view,
   and peace one can't ignore?

Is this the Volga? Don't forget.
   Or sacred Ganges' flow?
Or Rio Grande, I owe a debt
   for songs some of us know?

Is this the Rhine that's flowing north
   with mystic Lorelei
releasing such a tempest forth
   shipwrecks cannot belie?

Is this the River Jordan's banks
   that line the Holy Land;
where saints of three great faiths give thanks,
   and love must take a stand?

Yes, any river it may be,
    if I imagine so;
they're all a part of history
    no matter where I go.

39. As Rivers Run

As rivers run, so runs the heart
    with wild or steady flow
of anger or the calmest start
    of love that one can know.

As rivers crest, flood waters rise,
    the waters flood the land.
When hearts o'erflow with selfish lies,
    all love is drowned or banned.

The danger of fierce rapids scares
    all who are trapped therein.
A troubled heart oft needs repairs
    to help one new begin.

Like constancy of river flow
    that river life sustains,
a faithful heart will always show
    there's love life in its veins.

40. Two Rivers

A tiny stream begins its flow
    from one of nature's springs;
it does not know which way to go,
    but bubbles, leaps, upswings.

It winds along a mountain way,
    as brooks and creeks join in.
They Mother Nature's plan obey
    a river to begin.

Down mountain slopes the river glides
    and widens every hour;
its crashing water soon divides:
    Euphrates/Tigris power.

41. An Ocean Wave

Hear each new wave crash on the shore;
    not one repeats the sound
of any wave that's gone before,
    no matter where it's bound.

Each wave has life that's all its own;
    each wave is quite unique:
whether it's scattered or windblown,
    its swells rise to a peak.

And finally, it reaches sand
    and vanishes from sight,
but oh, it's life majestic, grand
    has thrilled me with delight.

42. Shifting Sand

A metaphor for life is sand
    for we shift to and fro.
On shifting sand, we oft can't stand
    and to the ground we go.

But there are moments quiet, smooth
    on sand at water's edge.
Each step we take secure, can soothe.
    It seems sand makes a pledge:

A pledge of solid ground on which
    with confidence we step,
but if sands shift and us bewitch,
    our walk becomes a schlep.

Our lives are like the shifting sand,
    sometimes we slip and fall,
but keeping balance, oh, how grand
    when we each spill forestall!

43. Surprise

Upon what seemed to be glazed glass
  the morning sunlight danced;
its rays and beams took turns *en masse,*
  as I looked on entranced.

What seemed glazed glass was the calm sea
  on which the sunlight played;
its dance was sheer delight, carefree,
  it colors vast arrayed.

Bright orange mixed with yellowed hue,
  as far as I could see,
lay gently o'er the sea's teal blue,
  a glorious color spree.

One moment I then looked away.
  Did all this I surmise?
Turned back and saw the same display:
  a dazzling morn's surprise.

44. What Does a Flower Mean?

What does a flower mean to you—
the red, the green or orange hue?
Its odor, does it mean much more,
the perfume that it has in store?
An amaryllis' diadem
is borne on a majestic stem.
A water lily floats about,
its beauty never is in doubt.

The buttercups at forest edge
or lined along a homegrown hedge,
welcome delight they are to see
with climbing plants known as sweet pea.
Sweet peas, how colorful are they,
for nature's best is on display.
Their fragrance, elegant, divine,
a gift of nature's choice design.

Rain forests offer such delight
by morning sun or moon at night.
A blooming vine upon a tree
casts beauty through its color spree
of green and red, colors so bright,
magenta hides beneath bright white.
In deserts, too, there is surprise
when flowers not there at rainfall rise.

Our world's a floral magic scene,
no matter where we might have been.
In nature, there's one thing that's free:
it's beauty on the land or sea.
The floral majesty it shares,
no thing, nothing with it compares!
So, treasure flowers, each blade of grass;
no thing earth's beauty can surpass.

Chapter 5

Nature's Gifts

45. Nature's Gifts

Oh Canada, how you amaze
    with breathtaking landscapes,
your mountain-tops with skirts of haze
    and waterfall escapes.

Your mountain-sides, some green, some bare,
    fuse meadows, flowing streams;
while arid spaces seem quite rare.
    Your beauty's made of dreams.

Your fir trees, cedar, poplar too,
    what pleasure to the eyes.
The tall ones, saplings all renew
    a hope that never dies.

46. An Enchanted Wood

Of wildlife, forests, wilderness
    enchantments we behold.
We hear their sounds, we see their dress,
    their wonders oft foretold.

A fairy tale's enchanted wood,
    a troll's bewitching style,
a prancing ghost-horse surely would
    remove a pleasant smile.

As I look out on forests green,
    are wonders I can't see
enchanting all just where I've been,
    each animal, each tree?

47. A Little Oak

The fir tree's green will never turn
    when seasons make their change,
but maple trees, oh how they yearn
    for colors of full range.

Their favorite seems bright red to be
    though orange and yellow too,
and if they're growing near the sea,
    a touch of brown will do.

Today I saw a group of trees
    whose name I do not know
but oh, does their changed color please—
    bright yellow all aglow.

But what about the little oak
    beneath the giant pines?
His sun is sparse, no rain to soak,
    because of giant vines.

How can he grow into a tree
    with giant roots and tall?
How can he be what he should be,
    follow the forest's call?

One day a giant woodsman came
    and changed his destiny.
He chopped down two trees, pine by name;
    a giant oak he'd be.

The sunlight warmed him day by day,
    the rains now gave him drink.
Come back some day and look, you'll say:
    "He's taller than you'd think!"

48. The Plains

The plains, the plains how vast they spread
    beneath the rising sun.
The wheat plumes glow a bright orange-red
    till morning rays are done.
As noon-time passes, colors change,
    orange-red to mellow gold.
When moonlight spreads across the range,
    bright fireflies then take hold.

The light-show Mother Nature sparks
    across the wide expanse
enlivens even meadowlarks,
    who join the fireflies' dance.
The dance that lasts till morning light
    across the plains appears.
Ballet of nature, what delight
    you dance through all the years.

49. The Oregon Coast

The winding coast of Oregon,
    its stunning cliffs and sands,
its scenes a magic paragon,
    its fertile rich farmlands,

its wide vast sands in sunlit gold,
    intrigue the sense of sight,
and native stories often told
    make sacred every site.

The stones, the boulders, bowing trees
    embrace the land with grace.
And everywhere one looks, one sees
    enchantment leaves a trace.

The blue-green sea with caps of white
    caresses the shoreline;
how easily one could delight
    to make of it a shrine.

A peace surrounds this glorious scene
    as nature wields her brush
to paint a memory where we've been
    and whispers, "Listen, hush."

50. Mount Kilauea

Mount Kilauea bursts with fire.
    Its lava fountains flow,
as Mother Nature shows her ire;
    each fissure sheds a glow.
The glow of orange lava's swath
    of lava-stricken earth
is seen in the volcanic froth,
    immense, immense its girth.

The blazing, red-hot molten rock
    and sulfur dioxide gas
have left Big Islanders in shock
    with threatening air mass.
The boiling pot of magma seems
    unendingly to burst,
and fissures multiply with streams,
    as if all life were cursed.

Is Mother Nature here at work
    or anger of the gods?
Or have we here, some natural quirk,
    and fate against all odds?
Eruptions, earthquakes both transpire
    without human control.
Destruction, death, and loss are dire!
    Dare one seek to console?

51. Wonder

The heavens and the seasons move
    at a deliberate pace.
Orion, Little Dipper prove
    they're not confined to space.

The sun, the moon, the stars, the sky
    move in an ordered plan,
and seasons change from wet to dry
    across the earth's wide span.

The wonder of this order seems
    too vast to understand:
Aurora borealis beams
    its multi-colored band.

The earth upon its axis spins
    in our galaxy's space,
a burst of shooting stars begins
    and ends without a trace.

More wondrous yet, a single soul
    through human eyes may see
these wonders stretch from pole to pole,
    and think, "They're there for me!"

52. Mountains

To mountain-tops the eagles soar
    where fierce winds reign as king,
an avalanche puts out a roar,
    a frightening, deadly thing.

Some mountain tops with trees are spread
    and others capped with snow,
and some are barren, as if dead,
    there nothing seems to grow.

I love the mountain trails that lead
    through flora spring and fall,
and sometimes fauna pass with speed,
    some large and some are small.

To wander on a mountain trail
    is filled with much surprise,
a waterfall or fluttering quail
    rich colored by sunrise.

The quiet of a moonlit night
    the dance of shadows near,
with silver beams of brilliant light
    the moon then lets me peer.

It lets me peer through silent woods
    at things I might not see,
the owls' own quiet neighborhoods
    while resting in a tree.

Oh mountains, mountains, you're a gift
    of nature to us all.
Your summits, how our spirits lift!
    You're nature's constant call.

53. A Mixture of Colors

The sky's mixture of colors bright
    was filled with reds, magentas, blues,
and geometric lines in white
    embraced the rising sun's rich hues.

How breathtaking this color scheme
    that momentarily appeared!
As quick as lightning, it would seem,
    a mixture new of colors neared.

The sky can paint what I cannot,
    even though my color palette's vast.
I mix, stir, think, "Oh, I forgot,
    for sky colors can change so fast."

At least the imprint's in my mind.
    Remembering, oh what a gift!
I think it won't be hard to find
    a thought that gives my days a lift.

54. Nature's Birthday Card

The sky was dressed in blue and white;
the puffs of white clouds were like clumps
of scattered flour lying still on a baker's floor.
The blue was like freshly-made icing
to adorn a just-baked birthday cake.
Suddenly a flock of Canadian geese
formed a giant V across the sky;
I suspect for Victoria's birthday cake.
I walked along a gentle stream and turned
to see a sunset transform the blue and white
to a sky of orange-tinged delight,
as if mixed with sugar and honey,
just like a delicious birthday pudding.
It was nature's wondrous birthday card!

Chapter 6

Nature's Demise

55. No Autumn Time

Some countries have no autumn time,
    their desert barren wastes
long since are treeless in a clime
    which green life devastates.

Long, long ago the hills were filled
    with giant cedar trees,
but climate change plant life has killed;
    the cedars no one sees.

There were yet other trees whose leaves
    in autumn turned to gold.
They're gone and Mother Nature grieves,
    and weeps for days of old.

Now there's no hope, just barren land
    consumes the vast terrain.
No seedlings, water are on hand,
    and there's no hope of rain.

This is the fate of climate change:
    destruction is its creed,
which humans implement; how strange,
    ignoring nature's need.

56. Climate Change, a Myth?

When autumn came this year, I thought:
    We'll have at last relief.
In summer climate-change we fought,
    mean temperatures were brief.

Above one hundred ten degrees,
    the summer crops had died,
the population on its knees,
    while skeptics laughed and lied.

"There's no such thing as climate change,"
    some boldly truth denied.
From hurricanes' expanded range,
    we learn, ten thousand died.

"The soaring temperatures," some say,
    "the ocean's steady rise,
are simply Mother Nature's way.
    Most surely no surprise!"

We lost our crops, lost people too!
    With ice caps' slow demise,
even polar bears now are but few—
    their food, their life source dies.

While scientists from year to year
    the evidence explain:
that human error, it is clear,
    breaks nature's natural chain.

Example number one: Ozone,
    invigorating air,
our industries destroy, it's known;
    but skeptics do not care.

For profit and for sake of greed,
    earth's climate slowly dies,
the life-sustaining source we need
    with lies cynics disguise.

Will there be winter, spring next year
    and what of summer, fall?
Will loss of seasons cynics sneer?
    Will they have that much gall?

57. Global Warming

Will here there be no dew or rain,
    no bounty in the field?
The ozone layer bear the strain,
    since greed to sense won't yield?

Some industries for sake of gain
    care not if heat is trapped;
carbon dioxide with disdain
    around the earth is wrapped.

The northern ice cap slowly wanes,
    as fossil fuels peak;
an island nation scarce remains,
    as oceans, new heights seek.

The profit word is jobs, jobs, jobs,
    which people need to live;
but profit is the thing that robs
    of life and won't forgive.

So, practice common sense, restraint,
    and economic thrift,
of greenhouse gases learn restraint
    for nature is a gift.

58. Where Is the Rain?

Some plains today receive no rain
    for global warming's change
prevents the clouds that would regain
    the rainstorms on the range.

Where once the fields were filled with wheat,
    there's dust and arid soil,
and farmers' families cannot eat,
    no matter how they toil.

Think carefully, you fans of greed!
    The time may surely come
when you won't have the things you need:
    food, water just for some.

59. Which Trademark?

The rustling of fall's windblown leaves,
    a brook's soft rippling sound,
the raindrops' drip from rooftop eaves,
    how eloquent, profound!

An ocean wave's breathtaking crash,
    the water's swift cascade,
the after-calm without a splash,
    as if nature had prayed.

The rainfall on an old thatched roof,
    a duck's quack, a dog's bark,
provide us with the simple proof
    of nature's own trademark.

The human trademark nature knows
    it sadly can't remove,
when climate change stops rains and snows,
    brings floods, as science can prove.

The glaciers vanish in the north,
    the ocean levels rise,
the human trademark brings these forth
    and without compromise.

As industry and corporate greed
    both damage Mother Earth,
they leave it in such desperate need,
    the need of a rebirth.

60. Greenland, for You We Grieve

Greenland, Greenland, for you we grieve,
    your ice sheet's slow demise,
could it force polar bears to leave?
    Their ice home melts and dies!

There they have played year after year;
    there they have raised their young.
There they've caught fish without a spear.
    Yet, now there's a sharp tongue,

which says, "Greenland's in no danger,
    nor is the world at all."
A fool is always a stranger
    to truth, while icebergs fall.

Ten percent of earth's fresh water
    the ice sheet there protects,
A fool leaves his imprimatur
    and climate change rejects.

As Greenland's ice sheet melts away,
    sea levels yearly rise,
white bears will have no place to stay.
    Who will apologize?

61. Disappearing Ice Castles

    Ice castles trimmed in turquoise hue
        with regal parapets of white
    are mirrored in a sea of blue
        when northern sun returns with light.

    This year such castles are but few;
        they've melted, lost in waters warm.
    The rising temperature's the clue.
        Yes, global warming's done the harm.

    We need the ice sheets on the seas
        in nature's northern, wintry climes.
    Dispense with climate change reprise;
        dispense with climate change's crimes.

62. Suppose

Suppose the sky of stars were stripped,
    or oceans of their waters drained,
all trees were buried in a crypt,
    and nothing of earth's flowers remained.
How drab the world then left behind!
Would you in nature much joy find?

www.ingramcontent.com/pod-product-compliance
Lightning Source LLC
Chambersburg PA
CBHW051658090426
42736CB00013B/2440